MW01247541

# Advance Praise for
# *SHAKESPEAREWALIS*

William Shakespeare stripped human beings of dissembling masks, and put them on as well, on stage, in the play and in the play-within-the play. He dug into the psychology of kings, queens, soldiers, merchants and peasants. He was not divine. He did not have twenty-twenty vision and he treated some women characters as slaves, possessions, prizes to be won. But he allowed the women to have their say in some scenes and always in the round.

This irreverent, saucy, ribald, and yet honest response to the overarching Will by four contemporary Indian and Sri Lankan women is a romp of a book, a joy ride in a stolen car with the sun roof down. Shakespeare gave us the car to drive to the end of experience. This time the drivers are women who have benefited from many centuries of tussling for power and influence between the male and female sexes. Will the warring finally stop? Will, I ask you, will we accept each other according to our bond/no more no less?

—**Indran Amirthanayagam**, author of
*Ten Thousand Steps Against the Tyrant*

# SHAKESPEARE *WALIS*:
## Verses on the Bard

FLOWERSONG
PRESS

poetry by

**Shweta Rao Garg**
**Sureshika Piyasena**
**Shashikala Assella**
**Ipsita Sengupta**

FLOWERSONG
PRESS

FlowerSong Press
Copyright © 2024 Edited by Sureshika Dishani Piyasena
ISBN: 978-1-963245-06-6

Published by FlowerSong Press
in the United States of America.
www.flowersongpress.com

Cover Image by Shweta Rao Garg
Set in Adobe Garamond Pro

NOTICE: SCHOOLS AND BUSINESSES
FlowerSong Press offers copies of this book at quantity discount with
bulk purchase for educational, business, or sales promotional use. For
information, please email the Publisher at info@flowersongpress.com.

# Foreword

This is a collection for our times – from four women poets who have taken on Shakespeare, their love, during the pandemic. The fact that they were in conversation with each other about a literary figure and his works, and worked towards this anthology is evidence that we humans (at least the women) can work together during the toughest of times, times that push us and lock us into our own individual resources. We have the capacity to overcome anything.

They show too that we the former colonized can also overcome our own colonization, read the texts the colonizers were excessively proud of, read our own resistances and appropriations, think through it all, and come up with an anthology of poems that demonstrate that we can critique that we love, accept the love even as we can read the contexts that gave us that love, celebrate the love with joy and irony and humour and clear-sighted acceptance.

The four Shakespearewalis, Shweta Garg, Sureshika Piyasena, Shashikala Assella, and Ipsita Sengupta, from two different countries (India and Sri Lanka), united by their education at the same university (Jawaharlal Nehru University, New Delhi), and their love for Shakespeare (which they must have developed earlier!), have their individual voices even if they write on the same topics. They write on women characters (with interesting twists – one making the boy actor 'come out' as Juliet), write on the 'twisted' men (of course), write (very appealing) appropriations, and in a final section called "Shakespearewalis to Shakespeare," in a series of very funny poems, they comment on his plays, his characters, his writing, and him!

But then all the poems in this anthology work as commentary on Shakespeare's works by four feisty subcontinental women who can see the humour in their readings and display it in verse and make you part of their literary journey. This is good poetry and good criticism. Shakespeare is in their good books and this book will be a good addition to the Shakespearean library, to read in good times and bad.

—**Professor GJV Prasad**

# Introduction

This collection is a result of our shared passion for Shakespeare and his world.

Sometimes we forget that William Shakespeare lived a few centuries ago, and that he was white, and was a man. We don't seem to mind that his characters speak the tongue of our oppressors. He is all ours.

After years of reading his plays, making love to his sonnets, failing auditions at the college production of his plays, learning his monologues by heart, even if they would get stuck in our mouths and come out in an accent he would have never understood; we love him.

We love him because he became ours. His Romeo and Juliet became our idols for adolescent love and his Caliban that of rebelling youth in us. We made him ours because he spoke to us, in a different tongue, but in the same rhythm as the iambs of our heartbeats.

Now with the awareness of the time and space between us, and armed with the coloniser-colonized discourse, and with feminist politics, we write verses on the world and words of the Bard of Avon. Some of these verses drip of love at his creations, others throw light, some throw pebbles at his injustices, while some verses are merely good-hearted jokes. Some build on, some dismantle, some undercut, some deconstruct – each of our verses give you, dear reader, an unpredictable ride into the corpus of William Shakespeare in unusual voices.

The contributing poets in this collection belong to one of the most maligned places of higher education in the current times. Our time at the then Centre of Linguistics and English (CLE) shaped us into the thinking-feeling individuals that we are now.

This project arose when we had re-connected, when our campus was under attack. We were distraught and felt helpless. We reminisced, we imagined a different future. And out of these imaginations, this project was conceived. We dived straight in and till the next year, we were churning poems on our WhatsApp group. The setbacks and losses during the pandemic dampened our attempts momentarily, but we always bounced back.

Our poems were never written in isolation, there was always a conversation around it. There was a generous give and take of ideas, of phrases and points of view. We nurtured each other's creative souls through daily inspiration and constructive criticism. It was a space of collective creation. There was a natural rhythm to our contributions. We realized when we checked much later, that we certainly had a method in our madness, i.e., we surely had some recurrent themes.

"Mad, Mad, Women" obviously has poems about the women characters of Shakespeare. We don't use the term "mad" as a pejorative, we reclaim the word, revel in its multiple connotations and read into the alleged madness. Lady M, Desdemona, Ophelia, Portia, Tamara etc. are all imagined anew. Does femininity have to be punished? We question why women were blamed for being themselves. We give voices to those whose stories were shrouded in darkness. We intend to break the stereotypes of mother figures, lovers, wives and daughters and celebrate wholesome women that Shakespeare's women aspire to be.

The "Twisted, Tormented Men" houses poems about the valorized men; the heroes apparent of the Shakespearean world. But what constitutes heroism? Why are these men so tormented, so twisted? Is masculinity a heavy yoke to bear? We scrutinize the vulnerabilities and entitlements of being a Shakespearean man from the perspective of our gender. Men are victims of the same structures that give them power and we try to highlight that in our verses.

We all love remakes and remixes. Creating something unfamiliar through the familiar is exciting. No doubt, the world is full of fanfiction. "Bad Spin-Offs" is about celebrating Shakespeare within the context of contemporary South Asian pop-culture. Some of these poems are fresh imaginings and critiques of the popular ones. We delve into films and create our own terse plots to show how Shakespeare is all around us in many avatars, and afterlives.

"Shakespearewalis to Shakespeare" is our direct address to the Bard. We taunt the Bard calling out his racism, sexism, and classism. The verses in this section aspire to right the wrongs of history and conventions even as there is a tacit acceptance of the impossibility of the task.

It is important that we also share the rationale behind the title of the collection. We were inspired by the Merchant Ivory 1965 film *Shakespeare Wallah*. As we identify as women, we settled for Shakespearewalis. We are Shakespearewalis - we deal with Shakespeare as our ware, our craft and art.

We are not sore millennials cancelling Shakespeare, on the contrary, we work within the discourse, adding more layers to the palimpsest of Shakespeare studies. We hope that the poems are perceived and read as being both playful and critical. Above all, these poems are love offerings to the tradition of the Bard in the subcontinent. Our South Asian perspectives are braided into all our poems alongside the original Elizabethan sensibilities.

These poems probe the universalization of Shakespeare's work by connecting it to the practices and politics of the present. In diversifying responses we also show, quite conversely, that Shakespeare could be universal for lending himself into these adaptations.

Finally, we would like to conclude that the readers need not be denizens of Shakespeare's world to visit our little globe created in this volume. The poems can be read, and we dare say, even be enjoyed, by those who are not familiar with Shakespeare's writings and those who parley with Shakespeare will get some newer aspects to ponder upon.

—**Shakespearewalis.**

# table of contents

## TWISTED, TORMENTED MEN

# BAD SPIN OFFS

# SHAKESPEAREWALIS TO SHAKESPEARE

# SHAKESPEARE *WALLS*:
## Verses on the Bard

# MAD, MAD, WOMEN

# Who Chooseth Me Must Give All and Hazard All He Hath

Daddy would choose
Who gets me
And my fat dowry
Something banal as death
Will not thwart his will
The lovers shall
Pass through
His game of boxes
Gold, silver, and lead
A metallic sieve
To strain out
The gem from dust
Love from lust
The pure from the rust
Daddy was concerned
His doll tried to be a person
Despite the rouge,
The curls, the corset
She could upset
The boat
The leaden caveat
A Fair warning
That the fair one
May wear her wit

A man's wig
And try to impress
The court.

**—Shweta**

# No Flowers for Ophelia

No Flowers for Ophelia,
The mind that drowned in sorrow,
A life spent controlled by men,
In death she put an end,
To all her woe-filled tomorrows.

Flowers she handed out,
Picking flowers for herself.
So the men can fight it out,
Over her grave once she was dead.

—Sureshika

# Lady Macbeth

I have no name
Like the witches,
The fourth witch
Just doing the dishes.
I'm a witch for helping
My husband
Would have been called a bitch
if I didn't.
I unsexed myself
To commit murder
But only got
a spot on my hand

That didn't disappear.

—Sureshika

# Will the World Call Me Wanton

Will the world call me wanton
Heedless and reckless
If I refuse
To drink this potion?
Because love from afar
And in sacred bowers
Is not enough,
When faced with death, debt

And familial wrath.

—Shashikala

# Lady Macbeth; or The Heady Mb App

You remember me
The haunting tone
That leapt outside
Flesh and bone, and weapons -
Words and womb
I fashioned to a tomb
To trip on, when unjoined.
What if I ride,
Dil se the time tide, and coin?
Not nursery rhymes, like those bitches in the grime
But whims, no not whine.

"Withhold him ....."
Thus Rilke spake to the beloved, the maid
And I did what he forbade.
Gathered memories, and made them into meme
Of a cult of instants
The Insta to Mb's sin,
Leashed love to his cower-courage
Or something akin.
Meant to be constant
And
Played the witch - the mother.
O the smother, the kick
The make-in-me of an app branded and
Hip - relaunched, host, pliant switch to his worth and wither,

Till rocked toy, phantoms, the suicided and forgot,
Or book of mirrors gather,
And metaphors mix
To fix -
A game at human futures
In a flick!

—**Ipsita**

# Nerissa

When my lady wanted to save
Her lily-livered husband
And his 'benefactor'
It was I who wanted to put
Some sense into her
But
Since you too decided to be there
Then I craved a glimpse of you
To see whether you carried
The same agony
In Bassanio
I came, I saw and I surrendered
To something akin to love

In a man's pants!

—Shashikala

# Cordelia

I am the third daughter
Cordelia
Disowned
For speaking the truth

Now as a wife
Still the third
Unable to go back
Unable to take back
That which was done
Undiplomatically
Truthfully.

Trapped in an unhappy marriage
To go back to an unhappy father
Or to stay on with an unhappy husband.
To go or not to go
That is the answer.

—Sureshika

# Desdemona

You all say I am pathetic
that I didn't fight,
But who would have thought
He wanted me to die?
Who kills another
Over a handkerchief anyway?
Besides I had nowhere to go,

I had run away.

It's easier to die

Than face society

After a failed marriage.

—Sureshika

# My Dearest Romeo

I loved you, not with a bleeding heart
Full of anxious agony
But in quiet
Quite an offhand manner
Because you thought you loved me
(Because men of your stature are hard to come by!)
Wishing, you had not come to see me
Masked, ambiguously recognisable
For I
With bated breath
Waited for

Mercutio.

**—Shashikala**

# Jealousy is a Green Eyed Monster

But I have bonny blue eyes
The eyes that beheld you
Beholding me, my love
I am more precious
Than all your Oriental loot
I am fairer than ivory
My smile, a fresh breeze
And yet I cease to breathe
Because of a stolen
Strawberry printed hanky

—Shweta

# Love No More No Less

"I love your majesty
According to my bond
No more no less"
Love, I shall withhold
Love I must reserve
To keep mine own intact
When scorned, shredded
By fathers once loved
By suitors once adored
I want my heart
Its pieces, tattered but
Mine
To be mine, till I heal.

—Shashikala

# Lavinia's Revelation

Father, I was raped
Not because I enticed them
I but walked, talked and breathed
Not because I taunted them
How could I
Being a mere woman.
I was raped when
My betrothed dragged me
When everyone spoke, but I
Had no voice
My tongue and hands were cut
Long before the hunt
Father, I was raped
When you decided to kill me
For dishonour brought to you
Father, I was raped
Not by one or two
But many
Including you.

—Shashikala

# What Kind of a Shakespearean Mum Are You?

## The Absent Mom

When you carelessly die
And let your children grow
With a wet-nurse, a morose
Husband, who only grows more
And the kids have
A tad bit more exciting life
They speak long winding lines
But when they (mercifully) pause
Their thoughts don't dwell on you
Or
When the weary debt ridden playwright
Doesn't bother thinking of speaking roles
For a middle aged man
Who would have played you?

—Shweta

# The Killer Mother

When you are given to
Passion, power trips
Penchant for perfumes
When you can throw a mewling infant
Attached to your boob
*"Out, damned child, out I say..."*
When you helicopter
Parent your man
Till he craps his pants
You pull out dagger and plant it on another
You empty the throne to throw in
Your first true child,
Your unquenchable desire
To bear the name
Of a Queen
But your stupid, spongy man
And the flotsam
Of your conscience
Wreak havoc. All the Elizabeth Ardens
Cannot sweeten that little hand.

—Shweta

# The Bridal Mother

When your sophomore,
Breaks from school
For his dad's funeral
But ends up feasting
At your wedding
He loses his shit
He strangely fixates
About your new husband
Fornicating you
He calls you
(and his girlfriend)
'Whores' in many words
Was he always so sexist?
You wonder
But you simper
Instead of shudder
You are the Queen
For f's sake
Enjoying a good lay
So late in your life
You would not stop
For that bigoted prude

—Shweta

## The Tigress Mom

You are the cautionary tale
Of the woman gone wrong
If given power
Will order rape
Torture for fun
Get her boyfriend
To kill her bastard son
The only way to stop
The Tigress Tamara
Is to feed her
Her Sons

—Shweta

# Miranda to Ferdinand

You appeared
In the image of my father,
I grew up
With master and slave
No female figure
Father called you another Caliban
And I defended you.
So I forgive you
When you cheat at chess
For that is love I was taught
To accept anything for a kiss.

—Sureshika

# Forgiving to Seek Revenge

Living, hiding
Denouncing my child, life and self
I lived, died and lived
For, Leontes,
Your forgiveness
Carries weight!
To live, will life.
I forgive you
Not for grand gestures
Not for your unworthy love
But
To live, breathe
And seek revenge
In my generous
Dead heart!

—**Shashikala**

# Gertrude

Hot flashes, flab
Fatuousness
Menopause makes
You reassess
Your life choices.
Should you have
grown it long,
your hair,
And tied your
Corset so tight?
Learnt flower
Arrangement
Over astronomy?
Smiled so often
Faked orgasms
Tolerated lifetime
Of tepid love
With a mild man
And ignored the
Man-child you bore
Who has turned out to be
Insufferable pedantic bore?

—Shweta

# To Tame, To Break

No food you said
Meets my standards
No hat or dress should be mine
Because you love me
More
You tame me, break me
Make me repeat
I repeat
The moon is the sun, a man a woman
To live.
Because
Bruises hurt, broken bones ache
And the heart
Bleeds every time, I swallow

My thoughts.

—Shashikala

# Rebecca's Faith

Daddy, I am sorry
Not for leaving my faith
Faith was but
Another shackle...
I can celebrate Christmas
As much as Passover....
Daddy I am not sorry
For eloping either
He promises a world
Of adventure and frolic
Love, even
Daddy I am sorry
Your old heart
Broke, together with
Your pride
shattered
Since that was
All we had.

—Shashikala

# Adriana Speaks

That's what we all do!
Put our fingers in our eyes and weep,
Desperately trying to keep,
Our husbands with us and with our children.
The wife should not have to be his mother.
Why is it only our duty to keep
The family together?

—Sureshika

# I am a Shrew

I am a shrew because I talk
I am a shrew because I think
I am a shrew, because I
Just, exist
I am a shrew, because
Taming a shrew
Can mean the world
To a
Man!

—Shashikala

# The Purgatory in Beatrice

There's no fashion but fashion in Messina.
Some wear faith, others a hat, a husband,
Gossip and gown,
Cuckold jokes, or the ancient algorithm around
Meat and appetite,
Waiting for wind and pluck.
What refuge, all's a bait ...

This game of words,
O aim so tame, matching matchsticks with him,
As forests singe within,
Voices gather, afterlives
And rivers on cinder-bed heave and sob,
Hounded by hurt, unhomed in a mob,
I play mar-maid, the Merry Maid masked in tongue,
Translator to the world,
On plague-pace, with permit.

I play to lose:
My heart, to Benedick/Tom-Dick-
Word-cannibals of the false dice,
Memories, to "all mirth and no matter",
Word, to stab-speak,
Truth, to men of other dyes
Who post-truth to police-fiction my ache, distance, Hero's vice,
Till, fermented in hides, my mouth stopped with a kiss,

I dissolve a-teared, naked
Unknowing mermaid - leaving nothing amiss.

**—Ipsita**

# Cleopatra

If it wasn't for his love
She would have ruled longer
But it is she who is called
the "gipsy," "The whore"
The "wrangling queen," "the Egyptian dish."

I,a mere boy
Playing this part
As a "Squeaking Cleopatra"
Stripped off these insults
When I assume myself again.

My male attire guards me
Off- stage against the insults
for a queen.
I step off and sigh
A sigh of relief
To be male again.

—Sureshika

# TWISTED,
# TORMENTED MEN

# Out of the Closet

At the Shakes-drama-comp
The audience applauds,
As I hold Romeo on stage
And we kiss.
This is my only moment
Out of the closet
When I'm accepted in a dress.

—Sureshika

# Bottom's Questions

Titania,
Would you have loved me
Had I not had donkey ears
Had you not had
The potion in your eyes
Had you not had a quarrel
Had I been normal?
Had I been
Simply Bottom!

—Shashikala

# Othello's Dilemma

You teach me
My skin colour is a curse
My speech gibberish
My history zilch
My people
You buy
You sell
You force breed
We are cattle
We are beasts
My sons pick your cotton
Build your place
My daughters suckle your babes
Make pancakes
Are repeatedly raped
You lynch us
Hoist us on trees
Your soldiers shoot us
At home, in cars
In streets

She with love
In her eyes
Skin all ivory
Embraces me
I can't breathe.

—Shweta

# Hamlet's Freedom

The dark wind
Howls at night
Screams 'freedom'
Creeps into my home,
Plays around and leaves laughing
At how freedom is so near for me
But yet so far
Denied by the lack of courage
To reach out and grab it.

—Sureshika

# Ophelia, Allow me to Mansplain

*Know yourself a baby*
And I shall teach you
The trappings of a man's heart
*Know yourself a baby*
For even the best of knight
Shall want to die
To enter that which lies
Between your legs
*Know yourself a baby*
But you can bear a child
And you will be shunned
As the wanton wild one
And he shall marry
Where his daddy will decide
*Know yourself a baby*
You may be seen as a grown up
Only if your husband dies
Leaving your son too small
To handle your affairs

—Shweta

# Shylock's Heart

To be called
The cur, the wretch, the infidel
I smiled, and lent
My hard earned gold
To be called
The miser, the heartless, the unfaithful
I smiled, and lent
My blood, sweat and tears
To be robbed of
My pride, honour, wealth
I refuse, my daughter
But
I shall convert, ask for forgiveness, pay the price
Since my heart
Now is only
A bloodless pound of flesh!

—Shashikala

# To be or not to be

To be or not to be
That is the question
When faced with indecision
Rage, love and all other demands
Of duty, desire and defiance
I wish for a single ghost
to come and support
My wandering heart
That refuses to sleep

Coz of mothers, lovers and grief!

—Shashikala

# Loving Miranda

Hair, spun gold
Soft skin
Smooth smile
You, beloved mine
Miranda
I, Caliban
Love thee
In language yours
My wild heart
Sings
Storms, thunder, wild seas
An Island mine.

—Shashikala

# BAD SPIN-OFFs

# The Monsoon Rain

Shall I compare thee
To the monsoon rain?
Thou art bourgeois
And a torrential pain.

—Sureshika

# Romeo Miyan

Went to his barber for a trim
Got a head massage
Slick with mustard oil
Patted his wrists
With some jasmine attar
Stopped by the pan shop
Chewed the bloody betel
All the way from the market
To the gullie leading to my balcony
Romeo-Miyan tied up his lungi
Spat out his pan
Whistled,

"Oye, Juliet, meri jaan!"

—Shweta

# Temporary love

My man's smile is nothing like the sun
Sunshine is much warmer than his smirk
If men be nice, why then there are plenty more
If hair is a thing, he is slowly going bald
I have seen better women, who chase spiders
No such bravery I see in him
And in some men, the fragrance lingers
Than the musty smell of his old linen
I love his accent, but have known
Better and sexier accents from the same parts
I grant he is the first of his type
My man, but knows how to irritate
  And yet, I think we both know
  Love is temporary, passion even more.

—Shashikala

# The Woman Waits

All the world's a stage
And all men are players
And all women merely wait
As men bowl, bat, field,
Women are the bait
A man in his time plays many parts
But a woman waits
To be wooed
To be chased
To be proposed
She swoons
And gasps
And faints
But mostly, she waits.
The man, now a knight
Rides many horses,
Mares, even.
While she cleans, breeds, cooks
And waits
For her menstruation to end
For her man to descend into
Second childishness
Then she shall ride
A horse, or two, perhaps?

—Shweta

# The Hurley Burley

No sleep for this heavy heart
No balm for this hurt mind.
The dagger hangs in the air
Life is foul, but sometimes fair.
The daggers in their smiles
And false faces, hide false hearts.

—Sureshika

# The Disappeared

We make ghosts
Not the sheeted kind,
Regular Speare tribe
Of stalkers, routed mockers,
Or official toast,
That boomeranged
And stung a host -
Macbeth O - to harangues
In blank verse. Too harsh.
We speak in nursery rhyme

Of pulver chime.
Pound dust, rather must,
For the bullet we ricochet
And mistranslate, while being gathered into grime,
With melting parts - the Dogberry malaprop,
A Lavinia tongue, witch lullabies,
The underside, obscene blank hearse
Without alibis,
Unhomed allusions, we - the solvent
To final solutions.

Dishevelled the dark, we rune the ruins,
Reek limits to metaphors
Beat tattoos on true things -
Secured refrains/reports you know and all that
Devout bling -

Till tattoos black holes unsheathe,
Hathras, Khairlanji, JNU, Shiv Vihar
And all such proper names,
Engorged, called the heath.

**—Ipsita**

# The Plump Girl and Shakespeare

"Eh, what's her name, the plump one who talks"
Tasked Delhiwallah of taste, Shehzad, stage-gal,
Of dark and awesome, how entwined, her pal.

The plump one, flailing, upstream,
Exiled at home, bailed on rejects and a dream -
Bare sleep in pill

Hunger-eyes an eject in "English",
School and Shakespeare - trouble-baker, peer-spear,
Word as hole or heal

Finds instead the pachyderm a pet
On her T-shirt, words war unfeigned
Else in mask,
And Shakespeare a Hindustani seal
For the elect.

—Ipsita

# Goliyon ki Raasleela Ramleela

When they met
Their ideas of the Other
Shattered
The splinters pierced
Their kin
As they fell into
The deep end of love
The murderous lovers
Took quite literally
That love kills.

—**Shweta**

# R&J - short poem

It was just
An awful lot of raging hormones
lust fuelled deaths

—Shashikala

# The Winter's Tale

For five acts
A jealous fool
Kills, regrets and
Is forgiven
By the killed women

—Shashikala

# Taming of The Shrew

A woman
Who thinks and speaks
Is made
To die slowly

—Shashikala

# Haider

A murderous brother
A newly widowed bride
A son with filial pride
Something is rotten
In the state of Kashmir
Do we need anyone to tell us that?

—**Shweta**

# Lear

An old bat
Disappointed
At his favorite child's
Refusal to play a
Royal sycophant
Gives away the goodies
To the jerks
He fathered
Then they all get
Royally screwed
Ever after.

—Shweta

# As You Like It

A girl in disguise
Discovers freedom
Denied to her sex
As she flirts with
A man in the closet

—Shweta

# Wanted

Wanted:
An interracial couple
Non-stereotypical
Looking for a counsellor
Specialised in working with
Black broken men
And white women martyr

Wanted:
A poet to pen
Love poems
For fair maidens
Which are actually about them
And not the prick himself.

Wanted:
Women who could play women on stage

Wanted:
Men who can love other men on stage.
And women who could other women.

Wanted:
An app that filters Shakespeare out of his lines and translates to
English.

—Shweta

# All's a Stage

All the world's a stage
Where we wear our masks
And strut about
Pretending to be
Who we are not.

—Sureshika

# Fate

Was it written in the stars,
Or did the stars hide their fires?
The stars may have brought about my scars.
Do the stars fuel my desires?
I choose to defy them.

—Sureshika

# Shakespeare*walis* to Shakespeare

# Dear Will

Dear Will,
I swear by your receding hairline
Your eternal frown
Your pregnant belly
Your repugnant breath.
I swear by the wires
Sprouting out of
Your saucer-like ears
Your bulbous nose
Your sagging chest
The balding spot that
Glows like the sun
Under flickering night lamp
Your wrinkled skin
Packed with eye bags.
I am forsworn to all,
and I, too, think
*my love as rare*
*As any ~~she~~ you belied with*
*false compare...*

—Shweta

# Solo Flights

Your sonnets
forsake me
in the first few lines
my parts dismantled
cherry picked
to appropriate
your figures of speech
your sonnets
are about
you
loving yourself
rubbing your pen
swelling your pride
scattering your words
all over the world
and grunting at
your own ecstasy

your sonnet

—Shweta

# Your Will

To be your prize
The Bard deemed that I drank poison
Killed myself and the king
Broke my spirit
My vows, my heart
Died uselessly, crying to be
Accepted, understood, valued
While you strutted on
Making, becoming, unbecoming
Raving, merry making
On my trampled soul.

—Shashikala

# India in Shakespeare

Indian gems
Indian spices
Indian bed
An Indian kid
The apple of Titania's eyes
An apple of marital discord
Whom Oberon wouldn't stand.

Shakespeare came to India
In exchange of the gems,
The spices
Darn the bed,
The entire sodding land.

—**Shweta**

# Shakespeare in India

Shakespeare was a Brit
For thoroughbred Brits
White man's excuse
To oppress
The Empire's excess
Of the cultural kind
Shakespeare became brown
Too soon
When the coolies
Played him
In false accents
And discovered
A kindred
A weaver of tales
A dreamer of dreams
Given to hyperbole
And loads of baloney

—Shweta

# Reading Shakespeare in Sri Lanka

We read him
Sweating, swearing, anguish ridden
Swamped and cramped in our tiny
Tidy classrooms
Trying to imagine
Balconies full of masked lovers
hidden daggers and bawdy jokes on streets
And
Stolen kisses
While we sit
Legs together,
Dresses covering knees

—Shashikala

# Shakespeare Competition

All those posh accents
Expensive expansive emotions
Wrapped in amazing fragrances
Drown the tiny voices
The s and the b and the p
All mixed up
Still trying to play
The masque
Of The Tempest

—Shashikala

# Believe Me Verse

If you would have written
About the beauty of my heart,
Instead of the beauty of my eyes,
They would have not believed your verse.
I do not want to live in your rhyme,
Or live through a child of mine,
I will live by my own mind.

—Sureshika

# When Shakespeare Translated her to JNU

"Maqbool" bore her here, oh a trouncer she wrote,
Mumbai Macbeth whittled to entrance size,
Wondered at Stonehenge seats, unwieldy wrought,
Time-ride? story-eyed, talk-tea-in-stardust guise.

The place shook her apart, regrafted genes,
Rivered an unfinished make, asymmetries
Noded into birth and burn, crisp char-wince -
Played routes-turn-forest, in excess of metrics.

When dirt and star gathered to witness
And peacock sprung from branch to branch in sleep,
A moonmade steelscape quivered as slow press
To watch her wield the wilding way, on bard-boat, free-

Gathered to the dense-dyed accident, she
Chanted, "In an afterlife, let me thus, many-verse shaped be".

—Ipsita

# Hearts Return Home

I do not wish to be fair
But only fair to folks.
I do not wish to increase
Your desire or play to your desire to increase
My heart is mine to hold
I choose to give and withhold
A heart can be taken back
No it is not forever
Love is a feeling
Not a promise
If not handled with care
A heart finds its home elsewhere.

—Sureshika

# No Hunchback

Dear Will,
It was Scoliosis
Not a hunchback.
Next time get your facts right.
Thanks,
Richard III.

**—Sureshika**

# As You will, Will

I know to woo a woman
Because I am one.
I know that being persistent
Will make her run.
It is only I who could
Get through to Olivia,
She should have been mine but for trivia,
You made her marry Sebastian.
He's my twin, but not me.
What a shock for her it will be,
When she realises he only looks like me.
You rascal Will,
You will do
As you will.

—Sureshika

# About the
# Authors

**Shweta Rao Garg** is a poet, artist and academic from India recently relocated to Baltimore. A former Fulbrighter, her poems have been published in journals and magazines like *Indian Literature, Coldnoon, Everyday Poems, Alimentum Journal, Postcolonial Text, Transnational Literature, Muse India* etc. Her debut collection of poems *Of Goddesses and Women* was published by Sahitya Akademi in 2021. Her graphic novel, *The Tales from Campus: A Misguide to College* was published in 2023. She engages with Shakespeare in her paintings as well. Her series, 'Bard in Acrylic' is a reinterpretation of Shakespeare. Her artwork can be viewed at www.shwetaraogarg.com.

An accomplished poet, **Sureshika Piyasena** read for her PhD in English at Jawaharlal Nehru University, New Delhi, India. She has taught English Language and Literature at the University of Sri Jayewardenepura in Sri Lanka, City University of Hong Kong, and The Hong Kong Polytechnic University. Her poems have been published in the following poetry anthologies: *Skeletons*, *The Black Rose of Winter*, *Bridge of Fates*, *Greek Fire*, *Temptation*, *Shout it Out*, *Jeans: A Memorial*, and, *This House We Live In* as well as in *Misfit Quill* (e-zine), and *Primrose Road Poetry*, an online forum for poetry. Her debut collection of poems titled *Little Lost Loves* was published in May 2021 which is a chapbook on the theme of miscarriages and infant loss. Her second collection of poems is titled *Palimpsest* (2023).

**Shashikala Assella** completed her PhD from the Department of American and Canadian Studies at the University of Nottingham, UK and currently works as a Senior Lecturer and Head of the Department of English, University of Kelaniya, Sri Lanka. She has published her academic work on diasporic women's literature in many reputed collections and her debut poetry collection (manuscript) was long-listed for the Gratiaen Award 2019. This co-authored collection is her first contribution to an anthology while her other creative work (in prose) have been published in local dailies.

**Ipsita Sengupta** has studied life, literature and wonder at Jawaharlal Nehru University, New Delhi, from where she has an M.A. and PhD in English. She works as Associate Professor at the Department of English, Bankura University, West Bengal. A recipient of global interdisciplinary fellowships including the Australian National University Australian Studies Institute 2022-23 Visiting Fellowship, Ipsita has been a researcher of trans-studies, with research publications across India, Europe, Australia and the US on Indo-Australian connections, comparative studies, dialogue and translations between spaces and cultures and South Asian studies in books and journals of repute. Her occasional Bengali poems have been published in little magazines. *Shakesearewalis: Verses on the Bard* remains her debut poetic project in English.

FLOWERSONG
PRESS

FlowerSong Press nurtures essential verse
from, about, and throughout the borderlands.
Literary. Lyrical. Boundless.

Sign up for announcements about
new and upcoming titles at:

www.flowersongpress.com